THE FOUND DOG RIBBON DANCE

Dominic Finocchiaro

BROADWAY PLAY PUBLISHING INC
New York
www.broadwayplaypublishing.com
info@broadwayplaypublishing.com

THE FOUND DOG RIBBON DANCE
© Copyright 2019 Dominic Finocchiaro

Cover art by Natalie Khuen

First edition: June 2019
I S B N: 978-0-88145-828-2

Book design: Marie Donovan
Page make-up: Adobe InDesign
Typeface: Palatino

THE FOUND DOG RIBBON DANCE opened at the Echo Theater (Chris Fields, Artistic Director) in Los Angeles on 21 January 2017. Chris Fields and Jesse Cannady were the producers. The cast and creative contributors were:

norm .... Steven Strobel
dog .... Dan Hagan
dave .... Eric Gutierrez
norma .... Amanda Saunders
colt .... Gabriel Notarangelo
xeno .... Gregory Itzin
trista .... Clarissa Thibeaux
miranda .... Julie Dretzin
harrison .... West Liang

Director .... Alana Dietze
Costume designer .... Elena Flores
Lighting designer .... Jesse Baldridge
Scenic designer .... Kurt Wilson
Sound designer .... Gillian Moon
Dramaturg .... Isobel Bradbury
Stage manager .... Amanda Wagner

Large thanks to Columbia University, the National New Play Network, the Kennedy Center, Roundabout Theatre, the Seven Devils Playwrights Conference, PlayPenn, the Lark Play Development Center, and the Echo Theater. Even larger thanks to the amazing artists that worked on the play and helped it develop over the years—you give the work its heartbeat and its soul.

CHARACTERS & SETTING

dog, *any gender, any age*
norma, *female, late thirties-early forties*
norm, *male, early forties*
dave, *male, early forties*
colt, *male, teens*
xeno, *male, eighties*
trista, *female, teens*
harrison, *male, thirties-forties*
miranda, *female, thirties-forties*

a city in the pacific northwest
time: the present

NOTES

respect the ellipses.

punctuation is rhythmic, not grammatical. play it like music.

*on **dog**: both a dog and a human being, but more person than dog. explore. make choices, add barks. but keep it simple, and keep it honest.*

less is more. in design. in emotional expression. in everything.

on the cuddling: there are many different cuddling positions. experiment. there is a world beyond spooning.

*on doubling: if necessary, one actor can play **colt** and **harrison** and one actress can play **trista** and **miranda**.*

NOTE ON MUSIC

For performance of copyrighted songs, arrangements
or recordings referenced in this play, permission
of the copyright owner(s) must be obtained. Other
songs, arrangements or recordings may be substituted
provided permission from the copyright owner(s) of
such songs, arrangements or recordings is obtained
or songs, arrangements or recordings in the public
domain may be substituted.

Loneliness comes with life.
Whitney Houston

for my mother

(in one space, a man [**norm**], early forties, in boxers, an
undershirt, and a lucha mask holds a red ribbon and fiddles
with his laptop. in another, separate space, **dog** stands,
staring out at the audience. it is not a dog but a human being
wearing a t-shirt that says "DOG" on it.)

(the man turns on the camera in his laptop. turns on an
uptempo song, whitney houston's i wanna dance with
somebody or something similar. he begins a complicated
ribbon dance to the song. it is well-practiced and performed
with great fervor and dedication. maybe it is incredibly weird
and awkward, or maybe it is actually really kind of good.
dog continues to stare at the audience. the man finishes his
dance with a flourish. **dog** opens his mouth. a beat)

dog
...bark.

(the man fiddles with his laptop, turning off the camera. a
tennis ball rolls slowly across the stage in front of dog and
out of sight. **dog** watches it roll. looks back to the audience. a
beat. **dog** chases the tennis ball offstage.)

*

(**norma**'s apartment. **norma**, late thirties-early forties, and
dave, early forties)

dave
i've never done something like this before

norma
there's no reason to be nervous

dave
i don't think of myself as the kind of person that does

something like this

norma
what kind of person is that?

dave
i don't know
the not me kind of person

norma
that's not a kind of person
or that's a lot of kinds of persons

dave
do i pay you now?
or after?

norma
after is fine
take your jacket off
make yourself comfortable

*(from offstage, **dog** barks. he doesn't bark but actually just says the word "bark" loudly.)*

dave
is that a dog?
you have a dog?

norma
are you allergic?

dave
no, i just
it didn't say on the
i didn't know you had a dog

norma
i don't
i mean obviously that's a dog barking
but it's not mine

dave
dog sitting?

norma
i found him

dave
you found him?

norma
on the street
no tags or anything like that
but a collar
so it's not like he's just a stray
he's somebody's
just not mine

dave
and you just
and you just took him?

norma
what else was i supposed to do?

dave
aren't there people?
aren't there people to call?

norma
i wasn't gonna take him to some shelter
if you lost your dog, would you want him to end up in
some shelter?

dave
i don't have a dog

norma
but if you did?

dave
i've never had a dog
i've never had any kind of pet

norma
dogs are good companions

dave
are we on the clock?

norma
don't worry
i don't have any other appointments today
this is about getting to know you
this is about making you feel safe

dave
should i not feel safe?
is this a dangerous neighborhood?

norma
i was speaking on a more
on a more metaphorical level

dave
oh
so this is not a dangerous neighborhood?

norma
this is a safe neighborhood

dave
because i don't remember if i locked my car or not

norma
this is a safe neighborhood

dave
okay

norma
…

dave
what's your dog's name?

norma
it's not my dog

dave
what's not your dog's name?

norma
i don't know

dave
well what do you call it?

norma
i don't call it anything
i just found him yesterday
i haven't had to worry about it too much
been busy trying to keep him from tearing up the
  couch

dave
you could name him

norma
that wouldn't be right
he's not mine

dave
you could keep him

norma
he has a home
he has people that love him

dave
don't be so sure

norma
he has a collar

dave
what's a collar?
just some fabric
a collar's not a home
a collar's not people that love you

norma
maybe i shouldn't have brought him home in the first
  place
do you think i did the right thing?

dave
...

norma
...

dave
i think
i think if i were a dog
and i were lost
and alone
i think i'd be scared
maybe a little excited, but mostly scared
and i think if i was that dog
that slightly excited but mostly scared dog
and you showed up
and smiled at me
and took care of me
even for just a little while
i think i'd like that
i think i'd be very grateful
i think i'd be
i think i'd be something like happy

norma
...

dave
...

norma
...

dave
maybe i should go
yeah
i think i should go

norma
don't be silly
i'm glad you're here

dave
you are?

norma
stay
you can change in the bathroom

(after a moment, **dave** *exits to the bathroom.* **dog** *barks from offstage.* **norma** *talks to* **dog**.*)*

norma
shh
i'm working
what do you need?
i don't know what you're trying to tell me
just calm down
be good and i'll play with you when i'm done
i'll take you to the park
is that what your family does with you?
i'll buy a pack of tennis balls and we'll go
don't cry
we'll go to the park
i promise

*(***dave** *reenters wearing silly-colored pajamas with a silly design on them.)*

dave
i know
they're dumb

norma
they're perfect

*(***dave** *and* **norma** *move onto the bed.)*

norma
there are tissues on the bedside table
if you need them

dave
do people
do people usually need them?

norma
sometimes
it's good to let it all out
it's also fine not to
just know that they're there

dave
okay

norma
big or little?

dave
umm
little?
is that okay?

norma
of course

(**dave** *and* **norma** *spoon. she is big spoon.*)

norma
…

dave
…

norma
…

dave
how long have you been
doing
this?

norma
about eight months
i'm the first in the city

dave
how does one decide to become a
professional cuddler?

norma
how does one decide to become anything?

dave
what did you do before this?

norma
a lotta things
i was a yoga teacher
before that i was a netflix call center representative
retail, restaurants, all the rs
and i used to work in corporate, too
but that was years ago
feels like a different life
i guess i've done a little bit of everything
just not much stuck

dave
so why this?

norma
i guess i just wanted to find a way to help people
that sounds pretentious
like i'm curing cancer or something
but i think it's important
touch is
important

dave
...

norma
i'm babbling
we don't have to talk
we can just lay here
don't be afraid to go to sleep, either
whatever you need

dave
...

norma
…

dave
i think
i think just laying here
like this
i can't sleep
not without pills
but laying here like this
feels good
i think i'd like to just stay like this for awhile

norma
okay then
just like this
just like this

(**dave** and **norma** *lie there like that. for a long time.*)
*

(*coffee-shop.* **norm**, *early forties, behind the counter.* **norma**
holds a flyer.)

norm
i'm really sorry but
you can't put that
there

norma
why not?

norm
it's not me
it's just
company policy

norma
it's for a dog
it's for a dog i found

norm
i'm sorry
it's not
i don't

norma
there's a bulletin board
the purpose of a bulletin board
is to post bulletins
on the board

norm
that would follow
that would make sense

norma
what are these?
what are these bulletins?
what are these bulletins on this bulletin board?

norm
umm
that one looks like
guitar teacher
and that
that one
what does that one say?

norma
tarot
tarot readings

norm
that one's a dog walker
maybe you should take one
a little
stub thingy
maybe the dog walker can help you with your lost dog

norma
found dog

norm
found dog

norma
why can those people put up flyers
and i can't?

norm
i don't know
that's actually a really good point
that's actually a great point
there's a flaw in the system
there's a flaw in the
what's it called
protocol

norma
there is
it's a big flaw

norm
people didn't post those
when i was here
different shifts
different baristas
i'm just saying
i'm not like
i just do what they tell me

norma
but apparently
but apparently the other baristas
don't
and apparently it's not a problem
so
so unless there's
unless there's any number of
different protocols
for different baristas
it seems like there's an unwritten rule that's been

established
an unwritten rule that's been established as regards the
  bulletin board

norm
an unwritten rule that supersedes the written protocol
is that what you're saying?

norma
that's exactly what i'm saying

norm
i think i follow

norma
i think you do

norm
and
and for some reason
and for some innocent reason
and for some completely innocent reason i was never
  told this unwritten rule

norma
it's unwritten
maybe you were out of the room

norm
maybe i was in the bathroom

norma
maybe you were on a break

norm
it's unwritten

norma
simple enough

norm
so really
so really i'm actually breaking the rules
the unwritten rules

if i don't let you post your flyer
really i'm in the wrong

norma
not morally
but yes
as regards the rules
the unwritten rules
yes

norm
i don't like that

norma
of course not

norm
that's no good

norma
it's not

norm
what am i gonna do?

norma
i don't know
what *are* you gonna do?

norm
…

norma
…

norm
cute dog

norma
it is
he smells like fall
it's almost spring but he smells like fall

norm
like red leaves?

norma
like something like red leaves

norm
that's not a bad smell

norma
it's not

norm
…

norma
…

norm
go for it

norma
really?

norm
really
next to the dog walker
same target audience

norma
i like the way you think

norm
it's a cute dog
it deserves to be found
*

(**norma** *at the park with* **dog**. *rain. they throw the tennis ball. they actually toss the tennis ball back and forth to each other, like two people would.*)

norma
give it
i can't throw it if you won't give it back
this is what you guys like, right?
tennis balls, playing catch?
help me out here

give it
there, was that so hard?
my arm's no good
your mommy probably throws better
do you have a mommy?
and a daddy?
do you have brothers and sisters, too?
i never had brothers and sisters but i always thought
  it'd be nice
always someone to talk to
bark at
give it
good dog
oh, you're all muddy
i hate this rain
you don't seem to mind, though
you don't get lonely when the gray comes?
the gloom?
winter here's rough
you don't miss the sun?
guess not
yeah, i see you wagging that tail
if i had a tail i'd want it to wag all day long
i'd never want it to stop
because that means you're happy, doesn't it?
that means you're happy
and everybody wants to be happy

*

(**norma**'s *apartment.* **norma** *and* **colt**, *teens.*)

colt
he does tricks
have you seen his tricks?

norma
i don't know if it's the same dog

colt
picture looked the same
looked just like him
zeke
pretty fuzzy picture

norma
i'm not good with that kind of stuff
technology

colt
it's a photo
it's just taking a photo
anybody can take a photo

norma
my phone is old
flip phone
and i have a hard time
getting the pictures from my phone to my computer
luddite

colt
lud what?

norma
it doesn't matter

colt
i'm not stupid

norma
i didn't think you were

colt
i just don't use dumb words

norma
duly noted

colt
or say frilly shit like that
"duly noted"

that's not a thing people say
people read that
or see that in some show
some show set in like
england
with butlers
and tea
but people don't actually say shit like that

norma
but i just did
i'm people

colt
you're *a* person

norma
i wasn't implying i was multiple

colt
you're an exception
normal people don't say shit like that

norma
now i'm not normal?
duly noted

colt
can i just see my dog now?

norma
of course

(**norma** *exits.* **colt** *snoops around the room.*)

colt
what's with all these candles?
all this hippy shit?

norma
(o s)
it's for work

colt
you a what?
you a candle maker or something?

norma
(o s)
no
i'm a professional cuddler

colt
hah
that's funny

norma
(o s)
i'm serious

colt
i'm young, i'm not stupid

norma
(o s)
suit yourself

(**norma** *enters with* **dog**.)

norma
this him?
zeke, was it?

colt
kinda looks like him
kinda doesn't
zeke?
come, zeke
come

(**dog** *doesn't move.*)

colt
i don't know why i did that
zeke doesn't come when you call him
i don't know why i did that

norma
you said he could do tricks?
maybe try that?

colt
yeah, okay
that's a good idea
okay, zeke

(**colt** *goes to shake* **dog***'s hand, like two people would.*)

colt
shake

(**dog** *doesn't move.*)

colt
shake

(**dog** *doesn't move.*)

colt
dance, zeke
do the dog dance
do the dog dance, zeke

(**dog** *doesn't move.*)

colt
come on
i'll sing it for you, okay
i'll sing and you do the dog dance
(*he sings a ditty, or maybe beat-boxes—it's a practiced, in-depth routine.*)
come on zeke
don't be a limp dick
do the dance

(**dog** *doesn't move.*)

colt
it's not him

norma
are you sure?

colt
of course
zeke can't resist the dog dance
he's got the beat in his blood

norma
maybe he's just not in the mood

colt
he's always in the mood
it's not him

norma
i'm sorry

colt
…

norma
…

colt
…

norma
…

colt
it's okay
i hate that dog anyway
dances like a retard
this is stupid

norma
are you okay?

colt
what?
my nose is running
i have allergies
back off, lady
weird lady with your stupid dog can't even dance

i'm allergic to you
i'm allergic to this stupid dog

norma
i'm sure you'll find him

colt
fat chance
it's been weeks
what's he doing, pitching a tent in the park?

norma
…

colt
stupid grainy photo
we're in the 21st century, lady
learn some basic skills
fucking hippy

norma
…

colt
…

norma
…

colt
i just thought maybe
like crazier stuff happens, right?
i thought maybe
stupid
i'm not stupid
i have to go

norma
you're not stupid
and you'll find him
i have a feeling

colt
what, you a psychic or something?
is that why you have all the candles?
you into palms and cards and crystal balls and the
    future and all that shit?

norma
...

colt
wait a minute
is it true?
are you
are you really psychic?

norma
...

(**norma** *smiles a knowing smile—she's not a liar, but
omitting the truth in this one case couldn't hurt, could it?*)

colt
you have a feeling?
that i'll find him?
don't hold back on me now
i need to know
i
i miss him, okay?
i really miss him

norma
...

colt
...

norma
just keep looking

colt
...

norma
…

colt
okay
yeah
i can do that

norma
…

colt
…

norma
…

colt
he's actually a pretty good dancer
for a dog
i don't know why i said he dances like a retard
how many dogs you know got rhythm?
he dances amazing
*

(coffee-shop. **norm** *behind the counter.* **norma** *waiting)*

norm
white chocolate mocha?

norma
you remembered?

norm
white chocolate mocha
one less pump
sweet
but not too sweet

norma
not today
something

something different
i feel like something special

norm
what's the occasion?
your birthday?
your mom's birthday?
your dad's birthday?
got a new job?
quit an old job?
won the lottery?
quitting smoking?
taking up yoga?
moving?
your birthday?

norma
nope

norm
what then?

norma
just

norm
just?

norma
yeah

just

norm
just 'cause?

norma
just 'cause

norm
not to be confused with
just cause
although i'm sure you have just cause

to switch it up
your just cause being
well
just 'cause

norma
sure
something like that

norm
so what'll it be?

norma
surprise me

norm
(too loud)
go out with me

norma
is that a new drink?
is that hot or cold?

norm
go out with me

norma
is there caramel?
does it come with whipped cream?

norm
(word vomit)
i know you probably think i'm a loser
probably think i'm a loser to be working at a
   coffee-shop at my age
working at a coffee-shop at 41
42
you probably think i spend all my time on the couch
   being lazy
being a loser
doing what a loser does
and then i come here and i make coffee and i hate

    myself and i hate my life
but i don't
i don't hate my life
i love my life
i love making coffee
and i love doing other things, too
i dance
i'm a dancer
not, like, a professional
but i dance
for myself
i dance for myself
with ribbons
and a mask, a lucha mask
usually to the music of whitney houston
i love whitney houston
i believe in the power
of the music of whitney houston
i dance for myself with ribbons and a mask to the
    music of whitney houston
and i make videos of my dancing
and i put the videos online
and i have fans
thousands
hundreds
and i love it
i love dancing
and i love other things, too
i love making home-made bread
i love the smell of home-made sourdough bread in my
    oven
what else?
bar trivia!
i love bar trivia
i am good at bar trivia
but not in a weird too good way
i am just good enough at bar trivia

i have interests
i have hobbies
get to know me
go out with me

norma
…

norm
…

norma
…

norm
…

norma
…

norm
whatever happened with the dog?

norma
i still have him

norm
no luck?

norma
no
no luck
people come
people get their hopes up
and then their hopes get dashed
and they leave
and i stay
and the dog stays
it's painful
it's painful to watch

norm
…

norma
…

norm
so what'll you have?

norma
okay

norm
what?

norma
a date
funny word
date
like a piece of fruit
like a fig
fig, date
date, fig
yeah, i'll go on a fig with you
but just so you know
it's been a long time
since my last
since my last fig
not a big figger
i don't fig much

norm
neither do i
i almost never fig
i mean, not in a sad way
just in a
neither do i

norma
…

norm
…

norma

…

norm
i'm norm
by the way
probably should have said that before
that probably would have been more
appropriate

norma
hi norm
i'm norma

norm
hi norma

norma
norm and norma

norm
we're like the same

norma
but different

norm
yeah
but different
that "a"

norma

…

norm
vowels
vowel

norma

…

norm

…

norma
…

norm
but seriously
what do you want to drink?

*

(**norma**'s *apartment.* **norma** *and* **xeno**, *eighties.*)

norma
would you like some water?
some tea?

xeno
…

norma
strong silent type
okay

xeno
…

norma
you're not allergic to dogs, are you?
i have a dog
not my dog
but there's a dog
here
i should have put something on the website
was hoping he'd be gone by now
no luck!
i hope you're not allergic to dogs

xeno
…

norma
so what made you decide
to contact me?
never mind

you don't have to say
anything
this is your time

xeno
…

norma
would it be weird if i told you that you're the
the oldest
client
i've seen?
not that
it's not a bad thing that you are
older, i mean
it's great that you're old
oh god
i'm babbling
would you like to lie down now?

(**norma** *and* **xeno** *lie down.*)

norma
i could put on some music
if you like

xeno
…

norma
or just like this
the quiet is nice too
easier to synch up our breathing

xeno
…

norma
…

xeno
…

norma
you smell like cedar wood
reminds me of my grandfather

xeno
...

norma
he died when i was seven
not that i'm saying you
not that you're
i'm just saying
i'll stop

xeno
...

norma
it's just i had forgotten

xeno
...

norma
it's nice

(**norma** *and* **xeno** *lie there like that. for a long time.*)
*

(*a restaurant.* **norm** *and* **norma**.)

norm
i tried okcupid
is that okay?
to admit?
are people admitting that now?

norma
it's okay to admit
i never have
tried it
i would
i just haven't

norm
i didn't like it
didn't like messaging people
felt weird
"you like hüsker du!
i like hüsker du!"
why do i care if you like hüsker du or not?

norma
i don't even know what that is

norm
never knew what to ask
"what do you like to do for fun?"
idiot
and tone
tone is hard
on okcupid
online
in general
in life
in general

norma
tone is hard

norm
do you use a smiley?
do you not use a smiley?
what do you capitalize?
long message?
short message?
it's too much
it makes me anxious
but i mean
it's like
it's like where do you meet people?

norma
good question

norm
where do *you* meet people?

norma
do i meet people?
i mean
i meet people
obviously
i meet people every day
but, i mean, like, people
like, people people
do i meet people?
not through work
through friends?
i don't know where i meet people
do i meet people?

norm
...

norma
...

norm
...

norma
...

norm
(too loud)
i slept with someone
once
on okcupid

norma
oh?

norm
i don't know why i said that
it's probably not, what
first date material

norma
it's okay

norm
now you think i'm some kind of
like
i'm not
i'm not whatever you're thinking

norma
i'm not thinking anything

norm
i'm not some play the field on the town kinda guy
i like to stay home
and watch netflix
i like old sitcoms
like, actually old
like i love "i love lucy"
and "the andy griffith show"
and "the mary tyler moore show"
that's kind of newer than the others but
but when she throws her hat in the air
oh man
i like to stay home and bake bread and watch netflix
i'm not a play the field on the town kind of guy
it was a one time thing
i'm just letting you know
i wanted to share with you
be vulnerable
they say to do that on dates
i read that in a book i think
or maybe it was an article online
but it said to do that on dates
in a relationship
not that this is a relationship
yet
but it said to do that on dates

i was just trying to do that
but i think i didn't do it right

norma
…

norm
…

norma
…

norm
…

norma
is the fish good?

norm
i actually don't really like fish
i just ordered it because it seemed like the right thing
   to order
on a date
like
vegetarian seemed like maybe not manly enough
but red meat seemed too aggressive
and i hate chicken
on principal
so i got the fish
i might have overthought it

norma
…

norm
…

norma
…

norm
…

norma
i had a one night stand, too
once
one night

norm
really?

norma
a long time ago
in college
sophomore year
forget the guy's name
did i know his name?
yes
i knew his name
i think
i hope
bruce
ben
bill
buh buh buh
no
it's gone
or was it a d?
duh duh duh

norm
derek

norma
i hate dereks

norm
dean

norma
only dean martin

norm
dinosaur jr

norma
anyway
buh buh buh duh duh duh
sophomore year
drunk
obviously wasn't very memorable

norm
...

norma
was that oversharing?

norm
no
that was right
that was just right

norma
like goldilocks
i'm like goldilocks and you're one of the bears

norm
which bear am i?

norma
is there a good one?
a bad one?
or are they all just
just bears?
i don't remember

norm
...

norma
you're you
you're just you
that's which bear you are

norm
...

norma
…

norm
…

norma
dinosaur jr
that was funny

norm
i like that band

norma
me too

norm
twinsies

norma
…

norm
…

norma
…

norm
…

norma
…

norm
(*too loud*)
do you wanna go listen to dinosaur jr in my car?
*

(**norm**'s car. **norm** *and* **norma**. *dinosaur jr.'s* feel the
pain *is playing, or something similar. they kiss. it's their
first kiss. it can be a long kiss. it can be a short kiss. it can
be electric. it can be incredibly awkward. it can be silly. it*

*can be uncomfortable. it can be messy. and then it is over. as
quickly as it began.)*

*

*(**norma**'s apartment. norma and **trista**, teens.)*

trista
i'm not a lesbian

norma
this has nothing to do with sex

trista
i'm just saying

norma
the forms you signed
specify
that this is purely about
intimacy
and touch
platonic touch

trista
yeah, i know
i'm just saying
i'm not a dyke
or am i not supposed to use that word?
i'm just saying

norma
you
you are eighteen, right?
just for legal purposes

trista
last month
don't worry, i have money

norma
i wasn't worried
so you're a senior then?

trista
yep
go warriors
barf

norma
not a fan?

trista
is anyone a fan of high school?
except fucktards
do i look like a fucktard?

norma
i'm not sure what that is

trista
loser, maybe
geek, maybe
but not a fucktard
fuck fucktards
god high school
hate hard

norma
well it's almost over, right?

trista
yeah, sure
that's what everybody says
everybody says college'll be better
but that's just what they say, right?
people
old people
no offense
older people
i mean, in middle school they say high school will be
     better
in high school they say college will be better
in college they say real life will be better
it's all just a big trick

big trick to stop you from getting all emo and using
  your shoelaces to hang yourself
i mean, was college better for you?
than high school?

norma
maybe
it was a long time ago
feels like a different person
feels like someone else's story
someone else's home movie
does that make any sense?

trista
that's weird
you're weird
are you high?
can i have some?

norma
would you like some water?
some tea?

trista
no
i have a
it's stupid
i have a nervous bladder
i don't want to have to pee
when we
do people do that?
just get up and use the bathroom?

norma
of course
you don't have to feel as if there is any
right way
to do this
as long as you follow the rules outlined in the form

trista
yeah, of course
duh
i'm not stupid
i'm not some pervert
pervert weirdo loser fucktard creeper
you get a lot of those?
creepers?

norma
it's still a new field
sometimes there can be
confusion
but i've been pretty lucky

trista
guys ever get hard?
you ever feel their little peckers poking at you?
eww yuck eww

norma
it's natural
i just move away
let them understand
tactfully
that that's not what this is about
but it's nothing to be ashamed of
it's like a sneeze

trista
a boner's like a sneeze?

norma
it's not something you can control
we get so hung up on shame
it's just the body doing what it's built to do

trista
i don't know
i don't think a boner's like a sneeze

norma
(laughs)
maybe not

trista
i don't think i could do it
some stranger's body
so close to you like that
can feel their heartbeat

norma
that's kind of the point
have you ever heard of oxytocin?

trista
oxy what?
is that like oxycontin?

norma
it's a hormone
in the body
there are these receptors in your brain
that release it
when you're
close
to someone else
they call it the cuddle hormone

trista
you're joking

norma
i'm serious
it's been proven to encourage all kinds of things
empathy
trust
it's kind of a miracle

trista
so if your client gets a boner, they can just blame it on

the oxy whatever
is that what you're saying?

norma
what i'm saying
is that we all need
other people
that's what makes us human

trista
yeah, but i mean
i mean that's, like
that's like why people have families, right?

norma
…

trista
…

norma
would you like to lie down?

trista
yeah
sure
that's why we're here, right?
lead the way
down the rabbit hole
do we just?

norma
there's not a formula
you can take off your hoodie
if you're warm

trista
no, i
it's just
i don't
it's just
i have

on my
it's gross

norma
it's okay
this is a safe space
you don't have to be ashamed
of anything

trista
...

(**trista** *takes off her hoodie, revealing cutting scars all up
and down both of her arms.* **norma** *and* **trista** *get into bed.
silence*)

norma
you can get closer

trista
yeah, sorry, duh
(*she scoots closer. silence*)
do you get a lot of
women
clients?
or is it mostly men?

norma
would you be uncomfortable if i told you that you
    were my first?
or would that make you feel special?

trista
i don't know
is it true?

norma
yeah
but you don't have to feel self-conscious
there's nothing wrong with asking for what you need

trista
...

norma
…

trista
…

norma
…

trista
you're warm

norma
we both are

trista
it's nice

norma
it means we're alive

trista
and that's
that's good?

norma
yes

trista
...

norma
yes, i think it is

(**norma** *and* **trista** *lie there like that. for a long time)*

*

(**norma** *at the park with* **dog**, *playing ball. gray sky)*

norma
if you were a person
what kind of person would you be?
would you be a happy person?
would you feel
content

inside yourself?
i think you would
i think you'd be the kind of person
that'd always be smiling
every day
all day long
yeah
i think you'd take care of yourself
i think you'd know how to love
and be loved
i think you'd be giving
and gracious
in your love

(**norm**, *unseen by* **norma**, *enters with a brown paper bag of
food.*)

norma
i think you wouldn't be afraid
of anything
i think you'd just laugh it off
all of it
i think you would understand
what mattered
and what didn't
i hope you would
good dog

norm
(too loud)
i'm not stalking you
i swear
this
this is where i eat lunch
peanut butter banana
no crust
every day
i swear i'm not stalking you

norma
i don't think you're stalking me

norm
oh
okay
that's good
that's great

norma
…

norm
it's a nice park
family park
kids on swings
not that i, like
watch the kids on the swings
that would be weird
that would be creepy
i don't watch the kids on the swings

norma
…

norm
…

norma
…

norm
he's cute
cuter in person
less blurry

norma
one would hope

norm
can i throw the ball for him?

norma
i don't know
can you?

(**norm** *throws the ball over* **dog***'s head.* **dog** *gives* **norm** *the stink-eye, then begrudgingly goes to retrieve the ball.*)

norma
nice arm

norm
i used to play baseball
community league
i thought it would be a good way
to meet people
to make friends
i don't have a lot of
people
like that
but i didn't like the people very much
and everybody was married
everybody had kids
i quit after a season

norma
i joined a knitting circle once
couldn't handle it
i suck at knitting

norm
everyone was knitting
for a while
everywhere you looked
people just
going about their business
knitting
then it stopped

norma
went out of fashion

norm
you were just ahead of the trend

norma
got out when the getting was good

norm
cut and ran

norma
that's me, one step ahead of the game
that's not me at all
not at all
but it's nice to imagine

norm
…

norma
…

norm
can i take you out to dinner again?
i won't order fish this time
and i won't talk about sex
i promise

norma
…

norm
i'm not good at this
i haven't been on a second date in
i shouldn't say how long

norma
…

norm
…

norma
okay

norm
okay?

norma
yes

norm
...

norma
yes

norm
...

norma
...

norm
yay
*

(a restaurant. music plays. **norma** *and* **norm.** *they don't
say anything. they eat their food. they smile. they don't say
anything.* **norm** *takes* **norma***'s hand. they hold hands. they
smile. they eat their food. they don't say anything.)*
*

*(***norma***'s apartment.* **norm** *and* **norma.** **dog** *on the bed.)*
norma
would you like some water?
some tea?
i could put on some music

norm
that's okay
i mean either way is
i mean i'll have
sure!

norma
which?

water?
tea?
music?

norm
(*blurted out*)
we shouldn't have sex tonight

norma
excuse me?

norm
not that you were
i wasn't implying
i'm sorry

norma
is everything okay?

norm

it's not that i don't
want to
i really want to
it's just
i get
attached
easily
emotionally
it's been a problem
before
i don't want there to be a problem
with you

norma
i understand
i don't want that, either

norm
the last person i was in a
relationship
with

i thought things were going well
i asked her to move in with me
it was probably too soon
okay, it was definitely too soon
i never heard from her again
that wasn't fun
we met at the coffee shop, too
i'll stop talking

norma
it's okay
i like when you talk

norm
i'm nervous

norma
don't be
come on, lie down with me
just for a little while
it's nice to just be close

(**norm** *and* **norma** *move to the bed.* **dog** *shuffles over to the floor.*)

norm
is he mad at me?
i don't want him to be mad at me

norma
he's just pouting
you're stealing his spot

norm
are you gonna miss him?
when someone finally
when he's gone?

norma
he needs his family
i have no business taking care of a dog
i can barely take care of myself

norm
i think you do a pretty good job

norma
fake it 'til you make it

(**norm** *and* **norma** *lie down.*)

norm
so this is like work for you
i'm like lying on your desk right now
i'm honored

norma
you should be

norm
you didn't want an office?
cuddle central?

norma
why would i?

norm
i don't know
keep work and
separate

norma
it's not something that you clock in and out of

norm
what about safety?

norma
i can handle it
i'm good at my job
the best
not that there's much competition
not that there's any competition

norm
i'm not too shabby myself
i'm an all-star cuddler

varsity cuddler
i'll cuddle your socks off

norma
but then won't my feet be cold?

norm
then i'll cuddle them back on
i'll cuddle your socks off *and* on
i mean, unless you don't want to
probably sick of cuddling

norma
it's
different
when it's not a job
when it's with someone that
it's different

norm
…

norma
i almost forgot
what it actually feels like when

norm
what does it feel like?

norma
…

norm
…

norma
…

*

(**norma**'s *apartment.* **norma** *and* **dave** *in bed.*)

dave
it was a couple weeks after the divorce
i had to box up a lot of stuff

didn't have the room anymore
studio apartment now
and i'm going through some boxes
a lotta junk
old birthday cards, broken magnets, that sort of stuff
and i find this one photo
photo of my wife and me
ex-wife
on the beach
in silly swim suits
smiling from ear to ear
i find this photo
and i just look at it
for a long time
have the strangest thought
 "i do not recognize this man"
it isn't even anything about my wife
that's the funny part
not funny
that's the surprising part
it isn't me feeling sad or lonely or nostalgic about my
   wife
it's
"i do not recognize this man"
who is he?
he's
he's smiling
what is that smile?
and the eyes
that's not me
there's a
distance
something's changed
something's
gone
but i don't know what
i can't pinpoint it

or it's just too many things
it's just
everything
norma
…
dave
…
norma
…
dave
where do they go?
the people we
were
norma
…
dave
where do they go?
norma
…
dave
…
(**norma** *takes* **dave**'s *hand. they lie there like that. for a long time)*
*
(**norma**'s *apartment.* **norm** *and* **norma**. *in bed.* **dog** *on floor.)*
norm
i don't like to think about late whitney
it's too sad
no
i like to think about golden age whitney
the eighties
or bodyguard whitney

"i will always love you"
the greatest song ever written
especially the way she sang it
that voice rising over everything
and that smile
you see that smile and you think
there's nothing that's not possible
for her
i think that's why i like to dance to her
to feel that possibility
for myself
and when i dance, i like to imagine that it didn't end
    the way it did
for her
i pretend she just retired
i pretend she's somewhere quiet
maybe by a river
a lake
just her and her daughter
just her and bobbi kristina
and she's given all of it up
the celebrity, the media, all of it
and she's happy
in the quiet
by her river
by her lake
with her child
and sometimes
sometimes she still sings
but now it's just because she wants to
it's not for anybody but her
i like that story

norma
i wish you'd let me see you dance

norm
it's very personal

norma
i can just google you

norm
it's under a different name

norma
you have a stage name?

norm
i'll show you when i'm ready

norma
what will make you ready?

norm
when i know you aren't leaving

norma
...

norm
...

norma
...

norm
i see this look in your eyes
sometimes
sometimes when you think no one's watching
this faraway look
you go somewhere

norma
...

norm
where do you go?

norma
i'm not going anywhere

norm
people say that

it's easy to say that
but it's hard to do

norma
look at my apartment
i haven't moved in ten years

norm
you know what i mean

norma
…

norm
…

norma
i do
yeah, i do

norm
…

norma
…

norm
…

norma
it's been a long time
since i've had to worry about
since i've had someone that
that knew where i was
that wanted me somewhere

norm
…

norma
…

norm
…

(**norma** *gets out of bed.*)

norma
it's getting late
you should probably go home

norm
you never let me stay the night
i'd like to
i'd like to wake up next to you

norma
you shouldn't
the dog

norm
it's not about the dog

norma
…

norm
why?

norma
…

norm
…

norma
i

norm
…

norma
i just

norm
…

norma
i can't

norm

...

*

(**norma**'s *apartment.* **norma** *and* **miranda**, *thirties-forties,*
power-suit. **miranda** *on her bluetooth.* **miranda** *talks at the*
speed of light.)

miranda
honey, put the hamster down
put the hamster back in the cage
the hamster is to be looked at, not touched
i don't care what the hamster's name is, i care that
   you're holding it
your brother's older, that's why
that's not skin, that's fur
wash your hands
that's daddy's responsibility, not mommy's
mommy makes the money and daddy cleans the
   hamster cage
you don't have a wheel because you're not a hamster
mommy's signing off now
mommy's done with this conversation
(*she hangs up.*)
sorry
i never thought i would be one of those people
you know
one of those people with kids
plural
i never thought i would be one of those people with
   kid
singular
do you have any?

norma
just me
singular

miranda
lucky you
i'm kidding
i love my children very much
my husband, i'm not so sure
kidding
i love my husband very much
you're married?
i'm interrogating you
where is it?
is that wrong?
calling it "it"?
i hate animals
hate is strong
i'm not a fan of animals
the kids love them
have the hamster
had a turtle but it died
kids dumped him in cold water, whoops
had a rabbit, don't want to talk about what happened
    to her
have the dog
had the dog
then it goes up and missing
kids crying
i just want to grab them and scream
"this is not the epitome of human suffering!
there are little girls in africa with their little girl parts
    cut off
THIS IS NOTHING!"
but you can't say that to a nine year old
even i know that
i'm rambling
can i see it?
i'm not trying to rush you
it's just meetings
it's just work work work

it's just busy busy bee
don't know why my husband couldn't take care of this
doesn't this qualify as house husband duties?
he doesn't like when i call him that
house husband
i say what would you like me to call you?
stay at home dad?
he says not that
homemaker?
he says not that
he says we shouldn't be stuck on terms
he says we should create new terms
he doesn't know what he wants me to call him
he certainly knows what he wants me to call him in
    bed
i need a xanax

norma
i'll get the dog

miranda
you're a doll

(**norma** *goes.* **miranda** *closes her eyes and does deep
breathing exercises.*)

norma
(o s)
you're the first person that's called in a long time
i was about ready to

(**norma** *comes out with* **dog**. **miranda** *opens her eyes.*)

miranda
no

norma
no?

miranda
that's not it

that's not the dog
that's not our dog

norma
you said
golden mix
brown collar

miranda
that's not a brown collar
are you an idiot?
are you mentally challenged?
that's not a brown collar
that's
i don't even know what that is
but that's not brown
that's not a brown collar

norma
i understand why you're upset

miranda
i'm not upset
you're just wasting my time
you say brown collar
you take the time to make a flyer
a flyer with a completely blurry photo, by the way
you take the time to make a flyer that says brown collar
and then you bring me this
are you color blind?
i'm not upset
i just value my time

norma
are you sure it's not him?

miranda
am i sure?
am i stupid?
god, how did my day turn into this?
(she tries to deep breathe again. she closes her eyes and does

her mantra.)
i am capable
i am strong
i am in control
i am in confuckingtrol
(she breathes out. opens her eyes)
it's fine
it'll do

norma
excuse me?

miranda
if i go home empty-handed my kids'll flip
no amount of ice cream
no amount of therapy
no
this way at least i'll have something
to distract them
maybe pick up a collar on the way home
an actual brown collar
maybe they won't know the difference

norma
no
i'm sorry
but that's
it's not your dog

miranda
can i write you a check?
how much?

norma
it's not about the money
i'm sorry to have wasted your time
but it's not your dog
that's stealing

miranda
it's not your dog, either

it's nobody's dog
but when i give you this check
then it becomes my dog
that's how capitalism works

norma
that's not how i work

miranda
i can't let this day be a total wash

(**miranda** *grabs* **dog** *by his shirt.* **norma** *grabs* **dog** *by another part of his shirt. a tug of war*)

norma
he doesn't know you
it's not right

miranda
right or wrong is irrelevant
it's for my kids

norma
it's not your dog

miranda
…

norma
i wish it was
but it's not
it's obviously not

miranda
…

norma
…

miranda
i don't like to be told no

norma
…

miranda

…

norma

…

miranda

…

norma

…

(**miranda** *lets go of* **dog.***)*

miranda
i have to call my husband
tell him to get the kids ready
do some triage
it's not gonna help
you don't how much they love that dog

norma
i'm sure you'll find him
i'm sure he's safe

miranda
i don't care if he's safe
i care about my kids
i care about having to tell my kids
that boomer
that their beloved dog
that their best friend
is not coming home
is dead in a ditch somewhere
hit by a car eaten by raccoons dead
i have to see the look on my kids' faces
do you understand how hard that is?
to have to look into the eyes of the people you most
   value
the people you most love
the people you want to never suffer never hurt

and cause them pain?
of course you don't
holed up here
no husband
no kids
of course you don't

norma
(exploding)
that's not fair
i understand
believe me
you don't know anything about me
i was just trying to help you find your dog
you don't know my life

miranda
...

norma
...

miranda
...

norma
...

miranda
fuck

norma
i think you should go

miranda
fuck

norma
i said go

miranda
i heard you the first time
it's just

it's just i'm having a hard time breathing
right now
it's just i'm not sure i have the
capacity
for movement
at this exact moment in time
it's just i'm not sure i can make it to the door
without exploding into a thousand hundred million
   little pieces
i heard you the first time

norma

...

miranda

...

(**miranda** *cries out loudly, like an animal in a trap. but
only momentarily. then it is gone. immediately. as if it never
happened.* **norma** *and* **miranda** *sit together in silence.*
miranda *calls her husband. genuine*)

miranda
hi
yes
no
it's not the dog
i don't know what to tell you
of course i care
of course i'm upset
no
don't do that
don't put them on the phone
why can't *you* tell them?
what else are you doing?
i'm not bullying you
no we don't need to talk to dr. birnbaum about this
you know i deeply value and respect you
i'm very grateful for the sacrifices you've made

for this family
just
just please don't put them on the phone
please
just give me a few more hours
okay?
thank you
i love you
i love you so much
i love you so goddamned much
(she hangs up. silence)
can i pet him?

*(**norma** brings **dog** over. **miranda** pets him. she pets him
more and more. she rests her head on **dog**'s head. she closes
her eyes and breathes **dog** in.)*
*

*(the park. **norm** and **norma** throw the ball for **dog**.)*

norm
maybe we should keep him

norma
we?

norm
maybe you should keep him

norma
i couldn't do that

norm
why not?

norma
it wouldn't be right

norm
you've looked everywhere
you've done your duty

norma
i'm not equipped for that kind of responsibility

norm
you already have the dog
you could just make him yours
you'd make a great dog mom

norma
but what if i don't want that?

norm
you don't want that?

norma
i don't know what i want
it's complicated
it's another living being

norm
you love him
he loves you
if everybody loves everybody
what's the problem?

norma
…

norm
…

norma
good dog

norm
norma, i love you

norma
what did you say?

norm
i said i love you

norma
…

norm
…

norma
why did you say that?

norm
because i do

norma
…

norm
…

norma
…

norm
say something

norma
…

norm
tell me what you're feeling

norma
…

norm
i know it's soon
but

norma
…

norm
you don't?

norma
i'm sorry but
that
that word
is hard

norm
it doesn't have to be

norma
it's a burden
you think you love me
but you don't even really know me
what's my middle name?
where was i born?
what's my favorite ice-cream?

norm
tell me, then
tell me everything

norma
and then what?
we ride off into the sunset?
on elephants?
it's not gonna happen like that

norm
it doesn't have to be difficult

norma
what do you know about difficult?

norm
…

norma
…

norm
…

norma
listen, i
i am not a good person
to love
i am in no way
a good person
to love

norm
so?

norma
…

norm
…

norma
…

norm
do you think this is how i pictured my life?
at 42?
alone on the couch watching black and white sitcoms?
baking bread nobody eats?
ribbon dancing in my underwear and a stupid
i can't breathe in that mask
and it makes me sweat
and it gives me a rash
it gives me a rash all over my face
do you think i think i'm some big catch?

norma
…

norm
neither of us are good people
to love

norma
…

norm
so what?

norma
…

norm
…

norma

…

*

(**norma**'s *apartment.* **norma** *and* **dave** *in bed.*)

norma

…

dave
what are you thinking about?

norma
what am i thinking about?
i don't know
am i thinking about anything?

dave
i want to know what's on your mind
what goes on
inside you

norma
why?

dave

…

(**dave** *kisses* **norma** *softly on the neck. she sits up.*)

norma
dave
now now

dave
i can't help it

norma
now we both know that's not true

dave
you haven't felt it?
these past few months
something

growing
between us?

norma
i feel a lot of things
i'm a human being
if i didn't feel things
i'd be worried

dave
you know what i mean
there's something
here
something real here

(**norma** *gets out of bed.*)

norma
maybe we should call it a day

dave
i have time
i have more time

norma
we can make it up later
i think we should call it a day

dave
don't deny what we have

norma
you're my client, dave
this is a professional relationship

dave
sure, it started out that way
but it's become
something more
i can feel the way your body relaxes
lets itself go
while we lay here
in your bed

norma
it's my job

dave
not like that
and the way you listen to me
i mean really listen

norma
i listen to all my clients

dave
not just listen
but hear
really hear

norma
i'm good at what i do
i care

dave
exactly
you care
you care about me

norma
we need to take a step back
i should have been more aware of
i think we should cancel our sessions going forward
for the time being

dave
that's not fair

norma
until we
until we reestablish some boundaries
create a safe space again

dave
i don't want that
that hurts me
i'm hurt

norma
i think you should go now
i won't bill you for this session
i just think you should go
it's for the best

dave
why are you toying with me?
is this all just a game to you?
some kind of fucked-up power trip?
messing with people's emotions
making them want you, so you can
you're just like
no
i don't accept that
i refuse to accept that
i know you feel it too
you're just scared
you're lonely
it's written all over your face
don't be scared
please

(**dave** *goes to* **norma** *and kisses her full on the mouth. she tries to pull away, but he holds her too tightly.*)

norma
NO
STOP!

(the **dog** *begins barking. this time, he does not say the word "bark," but actually barks.* **dave** *holds* **norma** *even tighter and kisses her again, stronger. she knees him in the groin. he doubles over. she crosses the room, maybe grabs something to protect herself with. the* **dog** *continues barking.* **dave** *and* **norma** *stare at each other for a long moment, holding their breathe.* **dave** *begins to cry. loudly. bawling like a small child, snot streaming from his nose.* **norma** *watches, uncertain what to do. the* **dog** *continues barking.* **dave***

gathers his clothes in his arms. norma watches him. **dave**
looks at **norma** *one more time. she doesn't move. he goes
through the front door, leaving it open.* **norma** *falls to the
floor. the* **dog** *keeps barking.* **norma** *is visibly shaken. she
tries to hold herself together. the* **dog** *keeps barking. she
curls into a ball, covering her ears to drum out the sound.
the* **dog** *keeps barking.* **norma** *holds back tears. the* **dog**
keeps barking. **norma** *breaks.)*

norma
STOP
JUST STOP
ENOUGH!

(the **dog** *keeps barking.* **norma** *crosses offstage to dog. reenters immediately, dragging him by the shirt. he continues
to bark. she forces* **dog** *out the open front door, then slams
it shut. he continues to bark through the door. she rests
her head against the door, her body heaving. the* **dog**
*continues to bark. then, silence. she doesn't move. then, after
a moment, her head bolts up, her body as if electrified. she
realizes what she has done. she opens the front door. the* **dog**
is not there. she stares at the space where he was.)

*

(the park. night. **norma** *and* **norm**. *leash)*

norm
dog!

norma
dog!

norm
we should have named him

norma
i didn't mean for this to happen
any of this

norm
he's probably waiting at your doorstep right now

just wait, you'll see
we'll go home and he'll be sitting there
smiling

norma
no he won't
take this seriously

norm
i am

norma
dog!

norm
it's gonna be okay

norma
no it's not
nothing is going to be okay
nothing has ever been okay
nothing will ever be
okay

norm
…

norma
i told you i wasn't ready for this
now look what happened
now look what i've done

norm
it's not your fault

norma
who else's?

norm
nobody's

norma
…

norm

…

norma

i don't know what i'm going to do if

if

norm

you'll go on

that's what people do

norma

no

that's just what people think people do

people that haven't ever

norm

norma

norma

DOG!

norm

…

norma

…

norm

maybe he went back

norma

excuse me?

norm

maybe he went back to his owners

his real owners

you always said he wasn't your dog

norma

you're joking

norm

it's true

i mean

you spent so much time looking
this is what you wanted, isn't it?
to be rid of him?

norma
are you really that dense?

norm
...

norma
i didn't want
this
any of this

norm
...

norma
of course you don't understand
you've never had to take care of anything in your life
anything but yourself
you don't know what it means to actually
you don't know anything
about anything
except whitney houston
except some dead woman you never even met

norm
and you do?
i'm the only person you know that's not paying you
where are your people?
who are you taking care of?
except this dog
and look how that ended up

norma
...

norm
...

norma
…

norm
i'm sorry

norma
you should go
don't you have dances to make?

norm
…

norma
…

norm
…

norma
…

norm
norma
sometimes things just go
sometimes we don't
sometimes we don't get them back

norma
…

norm
you don't have to do this alone

norma
…

norm
…

norma
yes, i do

norm
…

norma
DOG!

*

(**norma**'s *bedroom.* **norma** *and* **harrison***, thirties-forties, in a suit, in bed. he fidgets*)

harrison
your sheets are itchy
what's the thread count?

norma
i'm not sure

harrison
…

norma
…

harrison
and these pillows
are they down or feather?

norma
i really don't know

harrison
what *do* you know?

norma
…

harrison
what time is it?

norma
you have time
just relax

harrison
i hate when people say that
"just relax"
when people say that

my whole body tenses up
"just relax"
"just relax"

norma
what would you rather me say?

harrison
…

norma
…

harrison
am i doing it wrong?
is it because i didn't bring pajamas?
i drank coffee this morning
should i not have done that?

norma
it doesn't matter

harrison
then what?
what's wrong?

norma
…

(**harrison** *fidgets. gets up*)

harrison
i knew this was a bad idea
but greg in i.t.
said i should try it
probably just fucking with me
fucking greg

norma
…

harrison
should have just gotten a massage
like a regular person

deep fucking tissue
fucking shiatsu
what was i thinking?

norma
just lay back down and we can talk a little bit
or i can turn on some music
light some candles
i have some nice aromatherapy oils

harrison
no
this was a mistake
thank you for your time
i don't know what i was thinking

norma
please
you have time
you still have time

harrison
and what?
your magic powers are gonna make me brand new?
you're gonna spoon me into feeling good?

norma
there are other positions we can try
breathing techniques
it can be an ecstatic experience

harrison
i don't even know what that means
i don't think you even know what that means

norma
it means
it means

harrison
…

norma
...

harrison
that's what i thought

norma
it means something

harrison
why are you even doing this?
doesn't seem like you enjoy it

norma
it's not about me
it's about you

harrison
i mean
if i wanted to cuddle with someone that didn't want to
    be there
i'd just call my ex-boyfriend

norma
this has never happened to me before
i swear
it works
it always works
it's supposed to always work

harrison
it's cuddling, not chemo

norma
i'm sorry
there's a lot on my mind
i've been having a hard time lately
i broke up with my boyfriend
and i lost my dog
not my dog, but
i lost a dog

harrison
i hate dogs
filthy animals

norma
he wasn't

harrison
shitting and pissing everywhere
and fleas
do you have fleas?
is that why your sheets were so itchy?

norma
dogs are good companions

harrison
no they're not
they're dumb
everybody thinks they're so smart
talking to them like they're people, like they
    understand
they have no idea what the fuck is going on
ever
no brains

norma
that's not true

harrison
i had a dog
when i was a kid
scout
dumb fucking dog
golden retriever shepherd something
took that dog everywhere
then it goes and bites the neighbor's kid
barely got her at all
just a nip on the cheek, big fucking deal
but my mom took him to the vet and that was that

bye bye scout
rest in peace, dumb dog

norma
…

harrison
what do vets do with them, after?
just like throw 'em in an incinerator, right?
no ceremony, tombstone, nothing
just throw 'em all in there
like big pieces of meat
just throw 'em all in there
until they're dust
until they're just
just
nothing

norma
…

harrison
…

norma
…

harrison
…

norma
will you lie down with me for a little while longer?
can we please just try again?

harrison
…

norma
…

harrison
do you really think it helps?
i'm serious

do you really think it does something?
anything?

norma

…

harrison

…

norma
i don't know

harrison

…

norma
i want to believe

harrison

…

norma
but i don't know anymore

*

*(in one space, **norma** searches for **dog**. in another, separate space, **norm** in his boxers and undershirt and holding his red ribbon, but without his mask. the song, whitney houston's i have nothing, or something similar. **norm** ribbon dances. **norma** searches and **norm** dances and dances and dances.)*

*

*(**norma**'s apartment. **norma** and **xeno**.)*

norma
i'm sorry the place is a little messy
i've been
it's been

xeno

…

norma
well
shall we get this show on the road?
i mean
not that
i'm not trying to rush you
i didn't mean
god, i can't do anything right

(**xeno** *climbs into bed.* **norma** *follows.*)

norma
…

xeno
…

norma
…

xeno
…

norma
i'm sorry
i'm a little tense
it's been a rough few weeks
i lost my dog
not my dog
i lost
and i broke up with my boyfriend
so yeah
a little tense
more than a little
i shouldn't be telling you this
any of this
this is not about me
this is about you

xeno
…

norma
…

xeno
…

norma
it's just
i'm starting to realize
that i'm not
good
at being
somebody's person
i'm good at
i think i'm really good at
being there
for people
i hope
i think
but being somebody's
person
isn't really about that
isn't really just about that

xeno
…

norma
maybe some people are just meant to be
alone
completely and utterly
that's okay, right?
there's nothing wrong with

xeno
…

norma
right?

xeno

…

norma

…

xeno

…

norma

…

xeno

…

norma

…

xeno
in the village of my ancestors
there was a single, solitary well
and every morning a young girl would go to the well
and she would collect the water for her family
and every morning a young man would go to the well
and he would collect the water for his family
and they would meet
at the well
and they did this
for many months
the season changed from spring to fall to spring again
but still they met
until one day
one day the young man asked for the young girl's hand
　　in marriage
and she was a very bold young girl
and she did not think about things like marriage or
　　family
she thought about things like swimming in the river
about things like listening to the wind and the little
　　animals in the trees
she was very stubborn

she was not easily swayed
and so she told the young man
"if you truly want my hand
then for the next one hundred days
take my pail
and fill it with water from the well
then carry it down the hill to my family's house
and i will take your pail
and do the same
and
if you do this
after one hundred days
i will be your wife"
and the young man was confused
"i don't understand
i am doing nothing for you
you will still travel as far
you will still carry the same weight of water
why is this what you ask of me, and not more?"
and the young girl smiled at the young man
and her smile was like no other
her teeth were big and white and her lips were the
   color of fresh blood
she smiled at the young man
and she told him
"there is no stronger vow of devotion
than to take another's burden as your own
and to let them do the same for you"
so the young man filled and carried the young girl's
   pail for one hundred days
and the young girl filled and carried the young man's
   pail for one hundred days
and after one hundred days
my grandparents were married
and the well is no longer there
in the village of my grandparents' birth
and my grandparents are no longer here

in this strange and precious world
but the story of the well remains
and the story of my grandfather and my grandmother
   remains
at least for a little longer
and that is enough

norma
…

xeno
…

norma
…

xeno
…

norma
…

(**norma** *takes a tissue from the bedside table. she is crying
silently. she wipes her eyes.* **xeno** *holds her tight.*)
*

(*the park. sunshine.* **norma**, *alone, with the tennis ball. she
throws it up in the air for herself. for a while. she lets it drop.
finally,* **norm** *enters.*)

norm
hi

norma
hi

norm
…

norma
…

norm
thanks for calling

norma
thanks for coming

norm
of course

norma
…

norm
…

norma
wanna?

(**norm** *and* **norma** *pick up the ball and throw it back and forth in silence for a while.*)

norma
keith

norm
…

norma
that was his name
that was going to be
his name
keith

norm
it's a good name

norma
…

norm
…

norma
…

norm
…

norma
…

norm
i miss you

norma
…

norm
…

norma
…

norm
…

norma
…

norm
…

(**norm** *and* **norma** *continue to silently play catch for a long while. then, norma speaks. quiet. simple. honest)*

norma
i was married once
when i was very young
and i had a child once
when i was very young
and i lost them both
when i was very young

norm
…

norma
and for a long time
i felt gone
out of my body
and then
when i finally came back

it was like something hadn't quite
made the return trip
and there was this
space
where that something used to be
and eventually you become used to it
the space
you find a way to live with it that is
safe
and
manageable
that gets the job done
and it's not living
but it's close enough
and you keep on at it
you keep almost living
until

norm
…

norma
…

norm
…

norma
until

norm
…

norma
…

norm
…

norma
…

norm
...

norma
...

norm
...

norma
...

norm
it's a nice day
summer's finally here

norma
...

norm
i love it when the rain goes
when the gray goes
they come back
of course they always come back
but
but we have a few months at least
of summer
before the rain
before the gray
before it all
we have a few months
here
in the sun

norma
...

norm

...

norma
...

norm

…

norma

…

norm

hi

norma

hi

norm

hi

norma

hi

norm

hi

norma

…

norm

…

norma

hi

end of play

www.ingramcontent.com/pod-product-compliance
Lightning Source LLC
Chambersburg PA
CBHW052128090426
42741CB00009B/2001